Wildland Fire Effects in Silviculturally Treated vs. Untreated Stands of New Mexico and Arizona

Douglas S. Cram, Terrell T. Baker, and Jon C. Boren

| Control | Lop & Scatter | Lop, Pile, & Burn | Harvest & Rx Fire |

Wildland Fire

| Control | Lop & Scatter | Lop, Pile, & Burn | Harvest & Rx Fire |

USDA Forest Service
Rocky Mountain Research Station
Research Paper RMRS-RP-55

February 2006

Cram, D.; Baker, T.; Boren, J. 2006. **Wildland fire effects in silviculturally treated vs. untreated stands of New Mexico and Arizona.** Research Paper RMRS-RP-55. Fort Collins, CO: U.S. Department of Agriculture, Forest Service, Rocky Mountain Research Station. 28 p.

Abstract

Stand-replacement fires, particularly in ponderosa pine (*Pinus ponderosa*) forests, have replaced high-frequency, low-intensity historical fire regimes. We examined whether forest stands treated recently using silvicultural practices would be (1) less susceptible to stand-replacing crownfires, and (2) more ecologically and functionally resilient compared to untreated stands following extreme wildland fire. Reports detailing wildland fire behavior in treated stands remain largely anecdotal. We compared fire severity indices, fireline intensity (btu/ft/s), stand characteristics including canopy bulk density (kg/m^3), and post-fire recovery indices in silviculturally treated vs. untreated forest stands in New Mexico and Arizona. Results indicated fire severity in pine-grassland forests was lowered when surface and aerial fuel loads were reduced. Specifically, as density (stems/ac) and basal area (ft^2/ac) decreased and mean tree diameter (in) increased, fire severity and fireline intensity decreased. The more aggressive the treatment (i.e., where the canopy bulk density was reduced), the less susceptible forest stands were to crownfire. However, mechanical treatments where slash was scattered rendered stands susceptible to near stand-replacement type damage when wildfire occurred within 4 years of treatment. On our study sites, mechanical treatment followed by prescribed fire had the greatest impact toward mitigating fire severity (i.e., aerial and surface fuels were reduced). Treated stands were also more ecologically and functionally resilient than untreated forest stands following wildland fire.

Key words: canopy bulk density, fire behavior, fire ecology, fire severity, ponderosa pine, silviculture

The Authors

Douglas S. Cram is a Research Specialist with the Cooperative Extension Service at New Mexico State University in Las Cruces, New Mexico.

Terrell T. Baker is an Associate Professor and Extension Riparian Management Specialist with the Cooperative Extension Service at New Mexico State University.

Jon C. Boren is an Associate Professor and Extension Wildlife Specialist with the Cooperative Extension Service at New Mexico State University.

Cover: Rodeo-Chediski fire 2002, contrast between lop, pile, burn (foreground) and lop and scatter (aft). Illustration by Jarod Lujan, Civil Engineer, Cooperative Extension Service, New Mexico State University. Photo by Doug Cram, Cooperative Extension Service, New Mexico State University.

Contents

Acknowledgments

This research was supported by the Rocky Mountain Research Station, National Fire Plan, USDA Forest Service, and New Mexico State University. The authors wish to thank D. Castro, A. Lujan, J. Lujan, G. Mason, L. Stavast, K. Wood (NMSU); B. Armstrong, L. Cole, J. Farley, J. Hamrick, T. Heim, J. Ingles, P. Klein-Taylor, R. Martin, D. Reisner, D. Watson, L. Wilmes (USFS); M. Hare (White Sands Forest Products, Inc.); D. Gutierrez (Governor of the Santa Clara Pueblo); S. Campbell (Arizona Cooperative Extension); and M. Coleman (Coleman Ranch) for invaluable help and assistance. In addition, the authors wish to thank J. Bailey, V. Baldwin, C. Edminster, D. Engle, J. Harrington, M. Loveall, and R. King for helpful comments and review of this manuscript.

Introduction

Low-frequency, high-intensity crownfires have replaced high-frequency, low-intensity fire regimes in southwestern pine (*Pinus* spp.)-grasslands. High-intensity crownfires can severely disrupt these forest ecosystems. Following high-intensity crownfires, timber resources are damaged or destroyed; wildlife habitat is altered or destroyed; nutrient stores are depleted; soil hydrology is altered; and duff, litter, and vegetation layers are removed exposing soil to rapid erosion events which in turn overwhelm riparian areas, streams, and rivers (Campbell and others 1977). In addition to ecological disruption, crownfires threaten lives, threaten property, and are notoriously expensive. The solution to reducing the risk of large-scale crownfires throughout the west is widely believed to lie in surface and aerial fuels reduction. However, information comparing fire behavior and fire effects on treated versus untreated forest stands following wildland fire remains largely anecdotal and unreplicated in descriptive studies. Further, there is some skepticism as to whether silvicultural treatments even reduce fire behavior. In light of the frequency, size, severity, and media coverage surrounding recent stand-replacement crownfires across the Western United States, the pendulum of past forest management is beginning to swing in a new direction. A new paradigm of "restoration" management has furthered this. Managers and an increasingly educated public question how effective silvicultural treatments are in reducing stand replacement fires.

Our study examined the effectiveness of recent silvicultural practices in reducing the severity and intensity of wildland fire. We hypothesized that silviculturally treated forest stands (<10 years since treatment) were less likely to experience crownfire and severe fire compared to untreated stands. Understanding the effectiveness of silvicultural treatments in reducing stand-replacement crownfire, as well as the ecological implications following treatment and wildland fire, was the rationale for this study. Silvicultural treatments examined included: non-commercial lop, pile, burn; non-commercial lop and pile; commercial harvest followed by prescribed fire; shelterwood; and untreated.

To ease communication and comprehension between the researcher and land manager, we use English units because most forest stand data is collected, analyzed, and spoken of in these terms. However, canopy bulk density is reported in kg/m³ because at the time of publication the simplest and most elegant method for calculating this stand index is with the Fire and Fuels

Extension to the Forest Vegetation Simulator (Reinhardt and Crookston 2003). Canopy bulk density estimates are given in metric units in this program.

Literature Review

Southwestern forests, particularly those dominated by ponderosa pine (*Pinus ponderosa*), developed under the influence of frequent fire (Sackett and others 1993). Reported mean fire intervals for southwestern ponderosa pine forests range between two to 12 years (Weaver 1951; Cooper 1960; Dieterich 1980). Over the last 10,000 years, frequent fire shaped vegetation composition, stand development, and structure in pine-grassland communities (Weaver 1943, 1964, 1967; Biswell 1959, 1972; Cooper 1960, 1961; Pyne 1982; Covington and Moore 1994). Frequent fires, characterized as light to moderately severe, were largely understory fires and killed few overstory pines. Fire acted as a natural thinning agent by reducing litter build-up, burning small trees, and thinning ladder fuels. Resulting forests were open and park-like with invigorated herbaceous understories providing the surface fuel for the fire cycle to repeat itself (Ahlgren and Ahlgren 1960; Moir and others 1997). Due to their open nature and lack of ladder fuels, stand replacement fires were historically uncommon in southwestern ponderosa pine forests (Woolsey 1911; Cooper 1960; Pyne 1996). However, a number of factors combined to change forest structure, understory and overstory composition, fuel biomass conditions, and the historic natural fire regime in southwestern forests over the last 120 years. Early contributing factors around the turn of the 20th century included logging practices (Habeck 1990) that removed overstory trees allowing for prolific conifer regeneration (Cooper 1960; Schubert 1974) and heavy grazing by sheep and cattle, which removed fine surface fuels necessary for fire spread (Baker and others 2004). Moreover, throughout the last 90 years fire suppression efforts and exclusion policies contributed significantly to extreme biomass fuel buildup as well as other ecological changes in these forests. Although early ecologists opposed to the 10 a.m. policy (the 10 a.m. policy was introduced and adhered to by the U.S. Forest Service in 1935; the policy stipulated a reported fire was to be contained by 10 a.m. the following day, and failing that, controlled by 10 a.m. the next day, and so on) and later others such as H. Weaver (1943) warned of increasing fire danger based on increasing biomass fuel loads due to lack of frequent surface fire, little attention was heeded. As a result, high-intensity crownfires have replaced

USDA For. Serv. Res. Pap. RMRS-RP-55. 2006

1

low-intensity fires in southwestern pine-grassland stands threatening not only those communities at the wildland-urban interface, but also the ecological integrity of vast areas throughout the West.

Early accounts in the fire literature comparing fire behavior between treated and untreated sites were anecdotal. Scientific rigor was deficient due to lack of empirical data, replicated treatments, failure to account for similar slope and aspect between the sites, and a general lack of statistical analysis. However, the general observation was reduced fire damage in recently treated sites (<10 years) as compared to untreated sites. Greater crown kill, tree kill, or charred bark height on untreated sites as opposed to adjacent sites treated with prescribed fire was reported by Moore and others (1955), Davis and Cooper (1963), Cumming (1964), and Wagle and Eakle (1979). Greater tree survival on mechanically treated sites with brush removal vs. untreated stands was reported by Van Wagner (1968). Fernandes and Botelho (2003) and Graham and others (2004) completed literature reviews of how prescribed burning reduced potential wildland fire hazard and how changing forest structure modified potential fire behavior and severity, respectively. Two recent empirical studies found (1) reduced fire severity on intensively vs. extensively managed stands following the fires in Yellowstone National Park in 1988, and (2) reduced fire severity and percent crown scorch on treated vs. untreated sites following prescribed fire, whole-tree thinning, and thinning followed by prescribed fire (Omi and Kalabokidis 1991; Pollet and Omi 2002; respectively). Recent theoretical studies have also predicted reduced fire severity following specific silvicultural prescriptions designed to reduce fire behavior (Scott 1998; Graham and others 1999; Fulé and others 2001).

Methods

Study Area

We visited all 11 National Forests in Region 3 (Arizona and New Mexico) during the summers of 2002 and 2003. In Arizona, we studied the Rodeo-Chediski fire in the Apache-Sitgreaves National Forest, and within New Mexico, we studied the Oso and Borrego fires in the Santa Fe National Forest (fig. 1). Data was collected on the Peñasco and Scott Able fires in the Lincoln National Forest (fig. 1), but site replication was not possible. Study sites within the Rodeo-Chediski fire were lower (6,430 ft) montane coniferous stands composed of ponderosa pine and gambel's oak (*Quercus*

gambelii). The Oso and Borrego fires burned in upper (8,120 ft) montane coniferous stands composed of ponderosa pine with some Douglas-fir (*Pseudotsuga menziesii*) and white fir (*Abies concolor*). The Peñasco fire burned in upper (7,595 ft) montane coniferous stands. However, the two study sites within the Peñasco fire differed in species composition and canopy cover (%) and were examined separately as Coleman One and Coleman Two. Coleman One was composed predominately of Douglas-fir and had a closed canopy, while Coleman Two was similar in composition to the Oso fire study sites, but had an open canopy. The Scott Able fire burned at a higher elevation (9,160 ft) within the upper montane coniferous forest and was composed of white fir, Douglas-fir, and spruce (*Picea* spp.) species.

Study Design

Due to the unpredictability of how, when, and where wildland fires burn, setting up an elegant pre-fire experimental design was impractical. The alternative to collecting and observing real-time fire behavior data on an *a priori* replicated experimental unit was to enter forest stands following wildland fire and collect data indicative of fire behavior. Although this is second in preference to real-time data on fire behavior, meaningful conclusions can be drawn. Replicated silvicultural treatments may exist on the landscape, but irregular burn patterns often complicate establishment of study sites. Finding adjacent treated and untreated study sites with similar slope and aspect was critical for comparison purposes. This criterion of similar slope and aspect on adjacent sites was particularly necessary to achieve scientific rigor. By accounting for the topography and weather legs of the fire behavior triangle (Pyne and others 1996:49) any differences in fire behavior could be attributed to differences in fuel (i.e., similar slope and aspect between experimental units accounts for topography, and because sites are adjacent our assumption was weather conditions such as wind, relative humidity, and temperature were the same between the two sites).

To advance our scientific understanding of how silvicultural treatments affected fire behavior beyond anecdotal, observational, and theoretical accounts, we concluded that empirical data from replicated treatments were essential. Meeting this treatment replication criterion proved to be difficult given the restraints of isolating the topography and weather legs of the fire environment triangle. To locate potential study sites a significant amount of time was devoted to contacting USDA Forest Service silviculturists at the forest and district levels, and in one case, a silviculturist from a

2

USDA For. Serv. Res. Pap. RMRS-RP-55. 2006

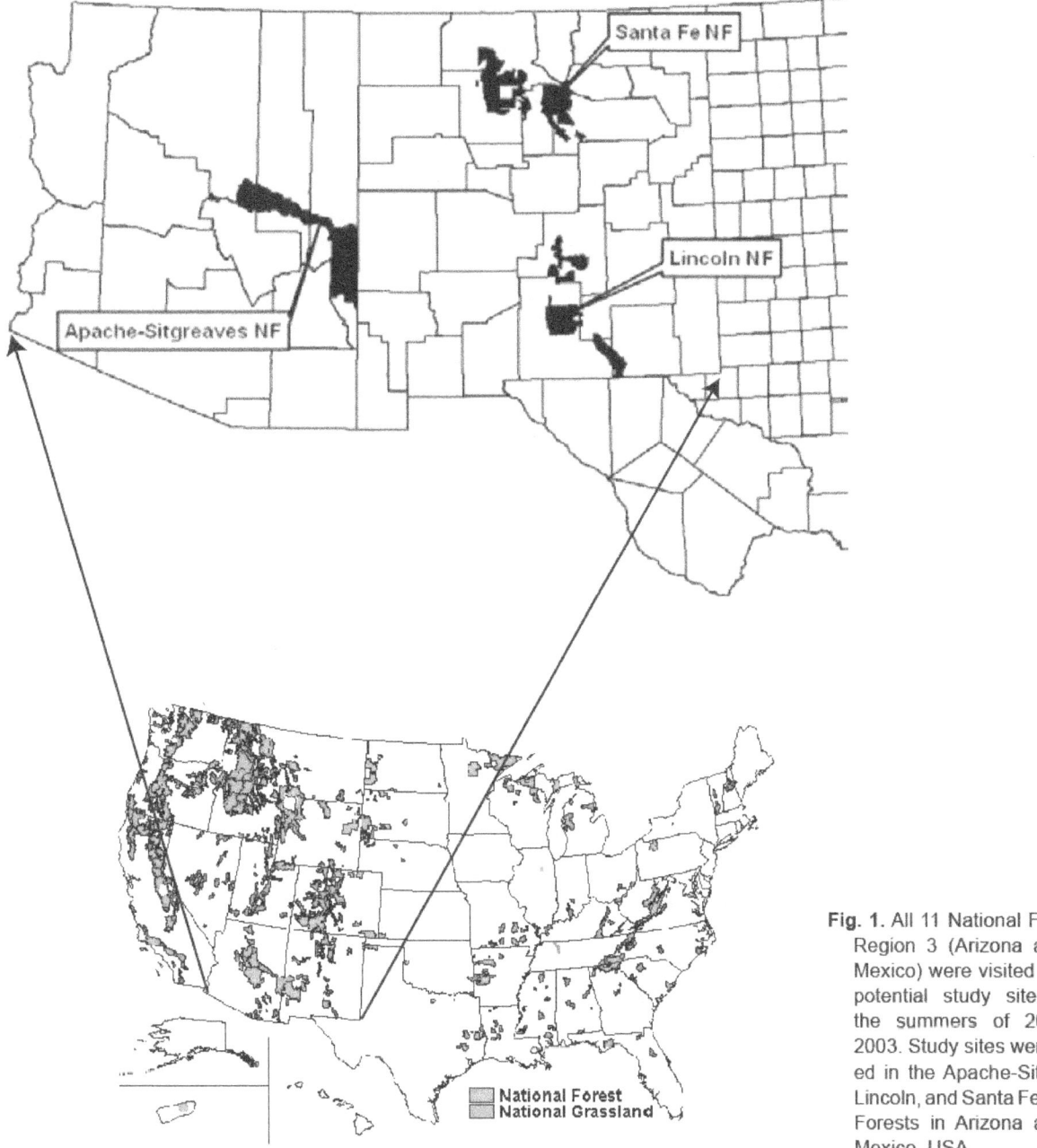

Fig. 1. All 11 National Forests in Region 3 (Arizona and New Mexico) were visited to locate potential study sites during the summers of 2002 and 2003. Study sites were selected in the Apache-Sitgreaves, Lincoln, and Santa Fe National Forests in Arizona and New Mexico, USA.

private timber company. Though time-consuming and logistically challenging, this effort proved to be indispensable as these individuals had knowledge of and access to records and maps surrounding recent and historic treatments. Geographic Information System specialists with the National Forests also provided maps with fire and treatment boundaries.

In each National Forest (except the Tonto) at least one potential study site (i.e., a silviculturally treated stand subsequently subjected to a wildland fire) was brought to our attention for inclusion and subsequent inspection (Appendix A). However, only three fire sites withstood

a conservative selection protocol: treatment and control sites had to have (1) similar slope and aspect on adjacent sites; (2) greater than 40 silviculturally-treated and untreated acres burned; and (3) no post-fire salvage cutting. The selection decision was generally easy to apply because so few sites met the first criterion of similar slope and aspect on adjacent sites.

Replicated study stands (fig. 2), defined entirely by management treatment within wildland fire boundaries, were > 40 ac. Specific stand treatment history and silvicultural prescription were researched and verified by consulting with the prescription forester (table 1).

USDA For. Serv. Res. Pap. RMRS-RP-55. 2006

3

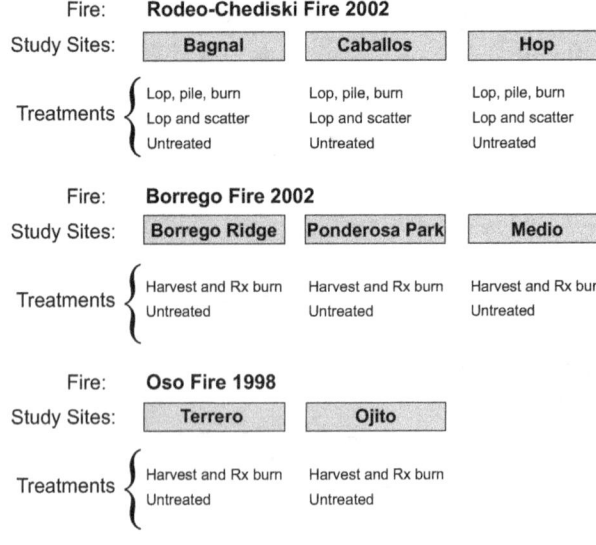

Fig. 2. Illustration of replicated treatments (*n* = 19) on the Rodeo-Chediski, Borrego, and Oso fires. Harvest & Rx burn is a commercial harvest followed by prescribed burn. Treatments on the Rodeo-Chediski Fire were non-commercial.

Stands had similar slope, aspect (table 1), and overstory composition. On the Borrego fire we located three replicates of two treatments in the summer of 2003 (*n* = 6):

1. Commercial harvest followed by prescribed burn;

1. Untreated.

On the Rodeo-Chediski fire we located three replicates of three treatments in the summer of 2002 (*n* = 9):

1. Non-commercial lop, pile, burn;

2. Non-commercial lop and scatter;

3. Untreated.

On the Oso fire we found two replicates of two treatments in the summer of 2002 (*n* = 4):

1. Commercial harvest followed by prescribed burn;

2. Untreated.

The silvicultural prescriptions for the Borrego and Oso study sites were designed similar to restoration treatments in terms of residual stand structure and fire reintroduction. On the Peñasco fire, two study sites,

Table 1. Study site characteristics in Arizona and New Mexico as measured in summer 2002 (Rodeo-Chediski, Oso, Peñasco, Scott Able) and 2003 (Borrego).

| | Fire, year, and stand name | | | | | | | | |
| | Rodeo-Chediski 2002 | | | | | | | | |
Characteristic	Bagnal			Caballos			Hop		
Treatment[a]	LPB	L&S	UT	LPB	L&S	UT	LPB	L&S	UT
Treatment year	1999	1999	NA	1999	1999	NA	1998	1998	NA
BA (ft²/ac)[b]	43	45	97	85	106	135	65	78	97
Elevation (ft)	6,453	6,453	6,453	6,729	6,729	6,729	6,650	6,650	6,650
Slope (%)	1	1	0	2	3	4	5	5	4
Aspect[c]	NA	NA	NA	NA	NA	NA	NA	NA	NA

| | Borrego 2002 | | | | | |
	Borrego Ridge		Ponderosa Park		Medio	
Treatment[a]	H&B	UT	H&B	UT	H&B	UT
Treatment year	1994	NA	1995	NA	1997	NA
BA (ft²/ac)[b]	54	109	64	108	61	71
Elevation (ft)	8,714	8,714	8,600	8,600	8,560	8,560
Slope (%)	10	10	9	4	8	9
Aspect[c]	NE	NE	W	W	W	W

| | Oso 1998 | | | | Peñasco 2002 | | | | Scott Able 2000 | |
	Ojito		Terrero		Coleman One		Coleman Two		Wayland	
Treatment[a]	H&B	UT	H&B	UT	THIN	UT	THIN	UT	Shelterwood	UT
Treatment year	1994	NA	1995	NA	1992	NA	1992	NA	1988	NA
BA (ft²/ac)[b]	48	114	55	106	60	128	14	127	30	134
Elevation (ft)	8,120	8,120	8,222	8,222	7,600	7,600	7,600	7,600	9,160	9,160
Slope (%)	3	1	2	4	2	1	3	4	15	13
Aspect[c]	NA	NA	NA	NA	NA	NA	NA	NA	N	N

[a] H&B = commercial harvest followed by prescribed burn; L&S = non-commercial lop and scatter; LPB = non-commercial lop, pile, burn; THIN = commercial thin; and UT = untreated.
[b] BA = basal area.
[c] Aspect not applicable (NA) when slope < 5 %.

Coleman One ($n = 2$) and Coleman Two ($n = 2$), were located. But because of different species composition and percent canopy cover between the two sites replication was not possible. Treated sites were on private property and compared to untreated sites on adjacent USDA Forest Service land. Treatments included:

1. Commercial thinning;
2. Untreated.

The Scott Able fire produced only one suitable study site ($n = 2$):
   1. Shelterwood;
   2. Untreated.

Because replication on the Peñasco and Scott Able fires were not possible, data from these fires were not included in the fire behavior analysis or results of this paper, but rather reported in table format in appendices B–F.

Fuel and Fire Weather Conditions

Fuel moisture conditions for the five fires studied were obtained through archives taken from the nearest (between 1–26 miles) weather station with the same elevation as the study site and on the same day the fire passed through the study sites. Timelag fuel moistures are reported to provide an indicator of fuel conditions leading up to the fire (table 2). Energy release component was also obtained to provide insight into conditions primed for extreme fire behavior (table 2). Energy release component is a measure of the potential heat released per unit area in the flaming zone of the fire and is affected by varying fuel moistures in the fuel bed. It has low variability on a day-to-day basis and is a good fire danger component for indicating the effects of

intermediate to long-term drying on fire behavior (Incident Response Pocket Guide 2004)

Stand Characteristics

Within five randomly located variable-radius plots per treatment we measured stand characteristics important to understanding fire behavior including basal area (ft^2/ac), density (stems/ac), diameter (in) at breast height (4½ ft), tree height (ft), crown length (ft), and height to pre-fire live crown (ft). Variable-radius plots were determined by using a 10-factor prism. Stem density and basal area were calculated following Avery and Burkhart (1994). Basal area measurements in treated vs. untreated sites provided an indication of the specific treatment prescription (table 1).

Canopy bulk density (CBD) (kg/m^3) was calculated using the Fire and Fuels Extension to the Forest Vegetation Simulator (FFE-FVS) (Reinhardt and Crookston 2003). The FFE-FVS defines CBD as the maximum 15-ft running mean of canopy bulk density for foliage and fine branchwood layers one-ft thick (Scott and Reinhardt 2001). Following Sando and Wick (1972), this method allows for the estimate of the "effective" CBD in nonuniform stands from a stand inventory that includes the following specific tree variables: species, height, crown ratio, and diameter. The FFE-FVS was used to estimate CBD because many USDA Forest Service personnel are familiar and trained in its use and manipulation, and thus they can easily calculate CBD using FVS-ready stand files. Unfortunately, at the time of this publication new empirical equations following Gray and Reinhardt (2003) for estimating canopy weights of western conifer species had not yet been integrated into FFE-FVS.

Table 2. Circumstance surrounding wildland fires studied in Arizona and New Mexico.

Circumstance	Fire				
	Oso	Borrego	Rodeo-Chediski	Scott Able	Peñasco
Date[a]	6/27–7/8 1998	5/22–6/6 2002	6/18–7/7 2002	5/11–20 2000	4/30–5/8 2002
Acres burned	5,365	13,000	467,064	16,500	15,400
ERC (btu/ft²)[b,c]	94	86	309	95	98
Timelag fuel moisture classes (%)					
10-hour	2	3	2	3	2
100-hour	4	4	2	3	3
1000-hour	6	7	3	5	6
Suppression cost					
(Million U.S. dollars)	3.5	Not available	43.0	3.6	5.7

[a] Ignition date to 100% containment date.
[b] As reported from closest weather station from day fire burned through study sites.
[c] ERC = energy release component.

USDA For. Serv. Res. Pap. RMRS-RP-55. 2006

5

Table 3a. Ocular estimates of surface damage following wildfire (modified after Ryan and Noste 1985).

Index value	Definition
0	**Unburned**: The fire did not burn on the forest floor. Some damage may occur due to radiated heat from adjacent areas.
1	**Light surface char**: Leaf litter charred or consumed. Surface appears black immediately after fire. Upper duff may be charred. Woody debris partially burned. Some small twigs and much of the branch wood remain. Logs scorched or blackened but not charred.
2	**Moderate surface char**: Litter consumed. Duff deeply charred, but mineral soil not visibly altered. Light-colored ash immediately after fire. Woody debris largely consumed. Some branch wood remains, but no foliage or twigs remain. Logs deeply charred.
3	**Deep surface char**: Litter and duff completely consumed; mineral soil visible. Structure of surface soil may be altered. Twigs and small branches are completely consumed. Few large branches may remain, but deeply charred. Sound logs deeply charred; rotten logs completely consumed.

Table 3b. Ocular estimates of crown damage following wildfire (Omi and Kalabokidis 1991).

Index value	Definition
0	**Unburned**: Fire did not enter stand.
1	**Light**: Surface burn without crown scorch.
2	**Spotty**: Irregular crown scorch.
3	**Moderate**: Intense burn with complete crown scorch.
4	**Severe**: High intensity canopy burn with crowns totally consumed.

Fire Severity and Behavior

We measured indices of fire severity and behavior including bole char height (ft), crown scorch height (ft), crown consumption height (ft), percent crown scorch (%), and percent crown consumption (%). To quantify fire severity, we characterized surface damage following Ryan and Noste (1985) and crown damage following Omi and Kalabokidis (1991) (table 3a and b, respectively).

Percent crown scorch and consumption were estimated ocularly. We used a clinometer to measure all heights. Evidence of residual buds on branches was used to identify branches that supported foliage prior to wildland fire. Unburned branches supporting foliage from surrounding stands were studied to provide visual calibration. The same individual made all estimates of crown scorch, consumption, and fire severity in both years of data collection.

Fireline intensity (btu/ft/s) was calculated using measured scorch heights and Van Wagner's (1973) equations. Because scorch height underestimates actual fireline intensity on unscorched or completely scorched trees, we followed Omi and Martinson's (2002) formula for calculating average scorch height. On untreated stands, fireline intensity $> I_o$ (the critical surface intensity required to initiate crowning) (Van Wagner 1977) was the variable of interest in this study.

Post-Fire Ecology

To characterize forest structure post-wildland fire we estimated percent cover following Brown and others (1982) in the following categories: grass-like, forb, shrub (0–3.3 and >3.3–6.6 ft height classes), litter, rock, bare soil, woody live stem, and woody dead stem (shrub >3.3–6.6 ft, woody live stem, and woody dead stem were omitted from table 6 due to lack of noteworthy cover). Percent cover for categories was estimated using Brown and others (1982) cover value scale. Dead and down fuel loading (lbs/ac), herbaceous fuel loading, and litter and duff depth (in) were also measured following Brown and others (1982).

Sampling Protocol

We measured fire severity indices (surface and crown damage) and post-fire ecological variables using four sub-sample plots around five variable radius plots in each treatment for a total of 20 sub-samples ($n = 5$). The first sub-point was the variable radius plot center. The second sub-point was located in a random direction 33 ft from the plot center. The remaining two sub-points were 120 and 240° from the second, and 33 ft from the plot center. To avoid bias from surrounding stands and an edge effect, no sampling was conducted within 165 ft of stand edge (Mueller-Dombois and Ellenberg 1974:123). All data were collected post wildland fire.

Table 4. Mean and standard error (SE) of forest stand characteristics and measured fire behavior indices important to understanding fire behavior as measured in New Mexico and Arizona National Forests, June–August 2002 (Rodeo-Chediski, Oso) and August 2003 (Borrego). Mode value is reported for surface and crown damage.

	Fire and treatment[a]												
	Rodeo-Chediski						Borrego				Oso			
	LPB		L&S		UT		H&B		UT		H&B		UT	
Variable	$\bar{x}$	SE	$\bar{x}$	SE	$\bar{x}$	SE	$\bar{x}$	SE	$\bar{x}$	SE	$\bar{x}$	SE	$\bar{x}$	SE
Estimated pre-fire condition														
Basal area (ft²/ac)	64	2	76	18	110	13	59	3	96	13	52	3	110	11
Diameter at breast height (in)	14	2	10	1	9	1	17	2	10	<1	18	1	9	1
Density (stems/ac)	119	14	190	48	831	461	60	25	883	282	45	10	491	89
Height to live crown (ft)	20	5	22	3	20	3	47	7	25	2	24	2	18	1
Canopy bulk density (kg/m³)	0.037	0.01	0.055	0.02	0.096	0.01	0.026	0.01	0.091	0.03	0.027	0.01	0.119	0.01
Fire severity														
Surface damage (0–3)	1		2		3		1		3		1		2	
Crown damage (0–4)	2		3		4		0		4		1		4	
Fire behavior														
Bole char height (ft)	8	4	29	4	36	6	12	1	37	3	10	1	36	1
Fireline intensity (btu/ft/s)[b]	140	61	288	28	500+	46	117	23	529+	59	53	11	586+	28

[a] LPB = non-commercial lop, pile, burn; L&S = non-commercial lop and scatter; UT = untreated; H&B = harvest and prescribed burn.
[b] "+" indicates underestimated fireline intensity.

Data Analysis

Reported means and standard errors for dependent and independent variables were summarized by treatment. Null hypothesis testing of treatment means was omitted in order to focus on magnitude of effect (Cherry 1998; Johnson 1999; Anderson and others 2000). Statistical Analysis System version 8 (SAS Institute 1985) was used for statistical analysis. Pearson Product-Moment Correlation Analysis was used as a starting point to index relationships between fire severity and behavior and stand structure characteristics, i.e., to what degree might a liner model describe the relationship between the two variables. Regression analysis was used to model relationships between fire damage and stand characteristics. Mallows' C_p statistic was used as criterion for model selection (Mallows 1964; Daniel and Wood 1980).

Results

Fire Severity and Behavior

Every treated stand experienced less severe crown damage as compared to the adjacent untreated stand (table 4, fig. 3). Surface damage was less severe on treated stands following the Rodeo-Chediski and Borrego fires

(table 4, fig. 3). Four years following the Oso fire, evidence of surface damage between treated and untreated sites was not statistically different. As would be expected based on crown and surface damage, calculations of fireline intensity were lower in treated than untreated stands (table 4). Actual fireline intensity was underestimated on every untreated stand because accurate measures of crown scorch height were limited by tree height, i.e., flame height exceeded the tallest tree. Untreated stands were more susceptible to complete crown consumption than treated stands (fig. 4). Height of bole char was also less on all stands treated mechanically and particularly those followed with prescribed fire as compared to untreated stands. Correlation analysis indicated the nature of the relationship between treated and untreated stands in terms of how fire severity and behavior related to stand characteristics (table 5, fig. 5). Crown damage (a discrete response variable) and fireline intensity (a continuous response variable) were positively related to basal area and density, and negatively related to average tree diameter (table 5). CBD was strongly correlated with surface and crown damage, and fireline intensity (table 5). The following regression interpretation assumes the presence of wildland fire, and in the case of predicting fireline intensity, crownfire is assumed. Regression analysis indicated that surface damage was best explained by stem density (surface damage: $y = -0.98 + 0.57$ Ln [density];

USDA For. Serv. Res. Pap. RMRS-RP-55. 2006

7

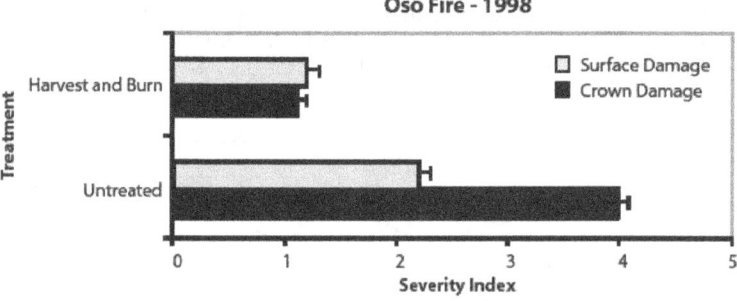

Oso Fire - 1998

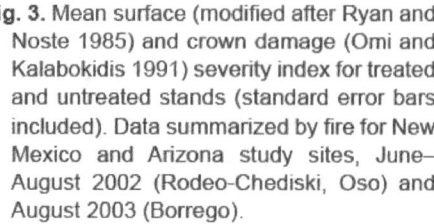

Fig. 3. Mean surface (modified after Ryan and Noste 1985) and crown damage (Omi and Kalabokidis 1991) severity index for treated and untreated stands (standard error bars included). Data summarized by fire for New Mexico and Arizona study sites, June–August 2002 (Rodeo-Chediski, Oso) and August 2003 (Borrego).

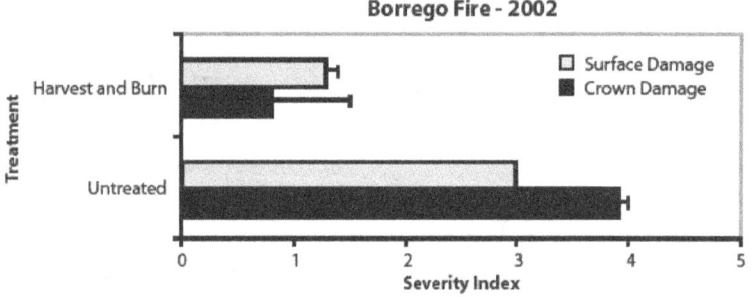

Borrego Fire - 2002

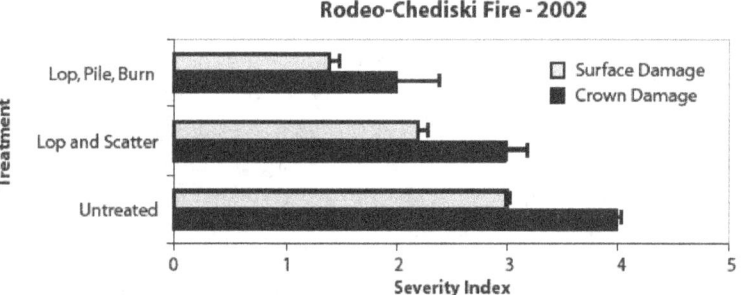

Rodeo-Chediski Fire - 2002

$r^2 = 0.79$), and crown damage was best explained by mean tree diameter and canopy bulk density (crown damage: $y = 4.2 - 0.2$ [diameter] + 14.9 [canopy bulk density]; $r^2 = 0.84$). Fireline intensity (i.e., > I_o) was best explained by CBD (fireline intensity: $y = 4.2 + 4040.3$ [canopy bulk density]; $r^2 = 0.78$). Although table 4 reports mean CBD, individual stand CBDs are of value in terms of identifying thresholds and therefore ranges are reported here: Rodeo-Chediski fire lop, pile, burn (0.031–0.047 kg/m³), lop and scatter (0.035–0.084 kg/m³), untreated (0.075–.111 kg/m³); Borrego fire commercial harvest and burn (0.018–0.039 kg/m³), untreated (0.052–0.118); and Oso fire commercial harvest and burn (0.016–0.037 kg/m³), untreated (0.109–0.129 kg/m³).

Ecological Effects—Understory

Four years following the Oso fire, grass cover remained greater in treated stands than untreated stands,

while bare soil remained higher in untreated stands (table 6). Following the Rodeo-Chediski fire, treated stands had greater litter cover and less bare soil than untreated stands (table 6). These differences were most evident between lop, pile, burn treatment stands (i.e., stands receiving the least degree of fire damage) and untreated stands. Following the Borrego fire, forb and shrub cover was greater in treated stands than untreated stands.

Immediately following the Rodeo-Chediski fire the lop, pile, burn treatment had greater herbaceous and litter loading as compared to untreated stands (table 7). One year following the Borrego fire herbaceous loading was also greater on treated stands as compared to untreated stands (table 7). Four years following the Oso fire only litter loading was greater on treated stands than untreated stands (table 7). Differences between residual fine dead and down fuel loads (1- and 10-hour fuels) on treated and untreated stands were negligible

8

USDA For. Serv. Res. Pap. RMRS-RP-55. 2006

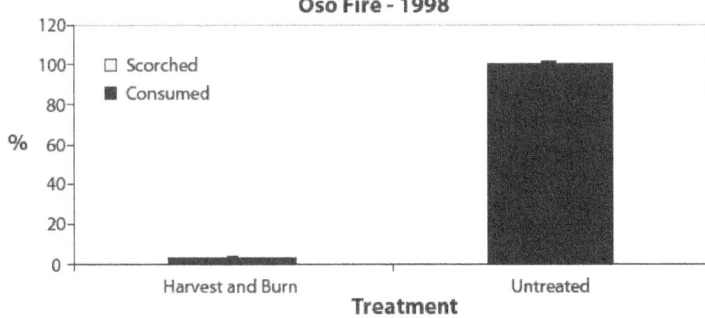

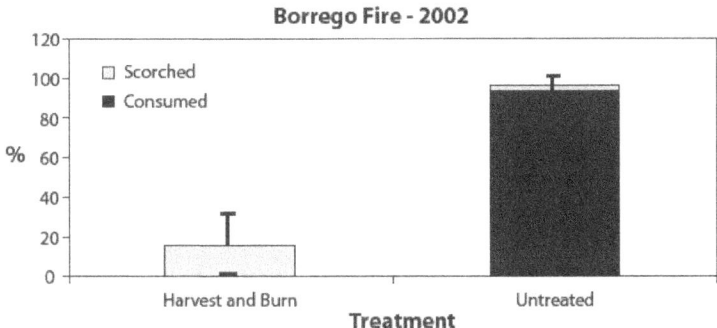

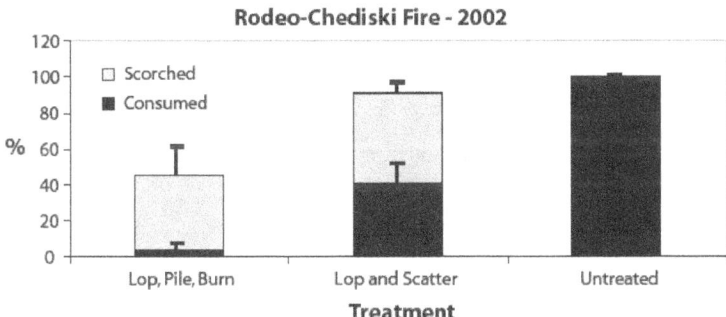

Fig. 4. Percent (%) of treated and untreated tree crowns scorched (i.e., needles remaining) and consumed (i.e., no needles remaining) by wildland fire (standard error bars included). Data summarized by fire for New Mexico and Arizona study sites, June–August 2002 (Rodeo-Chediski, Oso) and August 2003 (Borrego).

Table 5. Pearson Product-Moment Correlation coefficients between stand conditions and wildfire severity and behavior across all replicated stands (n = 19) in New Mexico and Arizona National Forests, June–August 2002 and August 2003.

	Fire severity index			
Stand condition	Surface damage index (0–3)	Crown damage index (0–4)	Bole char (ft)	Fireline intensity (btu/ft/s)
Basal area (ft²/ac)	0.73**	0.74**	0.73**	0.79**
Density (stems/ac)	0.67**	0.59*	0.39	0.56*
Diameter (in) at breast height	−0.80**	−0.88**	−0.68**	−0.75**
Canopy bulk density (kg/m³)	0.76**	0.84**	0.82**	0.88**
Height to live crown (ft)	−0.41	−0.61*	−0.24	−0.35

* $P \le 0.01$
** $P \le 0.001$

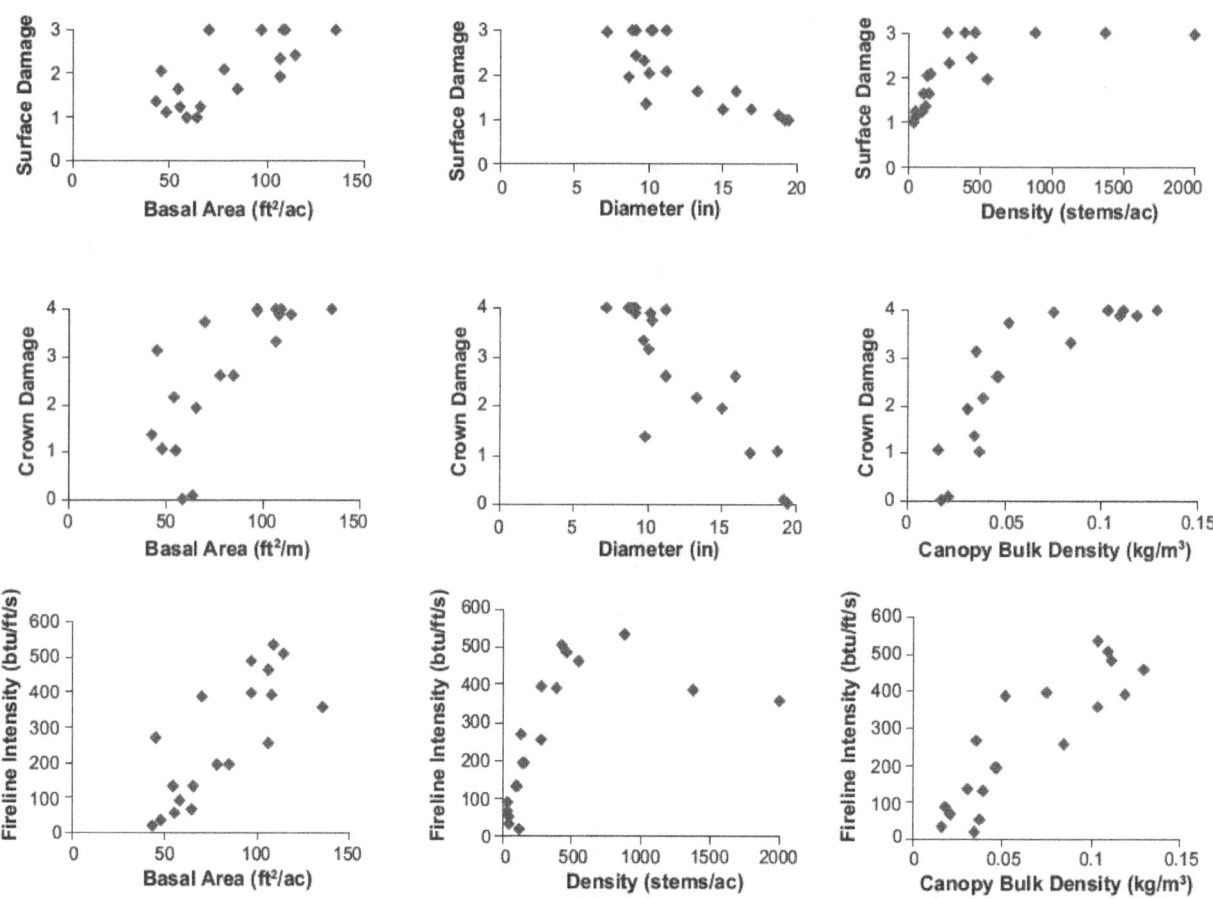

Fig. 5. Relation between mean stand characteristics, fire severity, and fire behavior for replicated stands (*n* = 19) in New Mexico and Arizona National Forests, June–August 2002 (Rodeo-Chediski, Oso) and August 2003 (Borrego).

Table 6. Mean and standard error (SE) of understory cover (%) response after wildland fire in New Mexico and Arizona National Forests, June–August 2002 (Rodeo-Chediski, Oso) and August 2003 (Borrego).

	Cover type									
	Grass		Forb		Shrub <3.3 ft		Bare soil		Litter	
Treatment	x̄	SE	x̄	SE	x̄	SE	x̄	SE	x̄	SE
Rodeo-Chediski Fire 2002										
Lop, pile, burn	2	0.9	1	0.9	<1	0.1	53	5.8	44	0.4
Lop and scatter	<1	0.1	<1	0.2	<1	<0.1	69	3.4	24	4.1
Untreated	<1	<0.1	<1	0.1	<1	<0.1	87	2.8	2	0.3
Borrego Fire 2002										
Harvest and burn	5	0.7	6	0.9	12	0.3	19	1.5	48	5.7
Untreated	4	0.9	2	0.4	3	2.2	68	8.6	15	0.8
Oso Fire 1998										
Harvest and burn	35	3.7	6	1.0	1	0.3	8	1.5	34	4.3
Untreated	4	1.3	11	1.8	4	0.7	34	5.5	21	2.7

10

USDA For. Serv. Res. Pap. RMRS-RP-55. 2006

Table 7. Mean and standard error (SE) of fuel loading and depth in treated and untreated forest stands following wildland fire in New Mexico and Arizona National Forests, June–August 2002 (Rodeo-Chediski, Oso) and 2003 (Borrego).

	Fire and treatment[a]													
	Rodeo-Chediski						Borrego				Oso			
	LPB		L&S		UT		H&B		UT		H&B		UT	
Variable	x̄	SE	x̄	SE	x̄	SE	x̄	SE	x̄	SE	x̄	SE	x̄	SE
Herb loading (lbs/ac)	12	1	5	1	2	1	306	59	107	23	348	42	172	21
Litter loading (lbs/ac)	1635	182	705	306	16	3	1,885	567	634	339	1,498	165	797	183
1-hr fuel loading (tons/ac)	<0.1	<0.1	<0.1	<0.1	0.0	0.0	<0.1	<0.1	<0.1	0.0	<0.1	<0.1	<0.1	<0.1
10-hr fuel loading (tons/ac)	0.1	<0.1	0.1	<0.1	0.0	0.0	0.3	0.1	0.1	<0.1	0.3	0.1	0.7	0.2
100-hr fuel loading (tons/ac)	0.5	0.1	0.2	0.1	0.3	0.1	0.5	0.1	0.2	0.1	0.6	0.2	1.5	0.4
1000-hr fuel loading (tons/ac)	0.4	0.2	1.3	0.2	0.3	0.1	5.7	2.2	0.9	0.4	1.5	0.6	7.9	1.8
Litter depth (in)	0.2	<0.1	0.1	<0.1	<0.1	<0.1	0.2	<0.1	0.1	<0.1	0.3	<0.1	0.2	0.1
Duff depth (in)	0.1	<0.1	<0.1	<0.1	<0.1	<0.1	0.2	<0.1	<0.1	<0.1	0.1	<0.1	0.1	<0.1

[a] LPB = non-commercial lop, pile, burn; L&S = non-commercial lop and scatter; UT = untreated; H&B = harvest and prescribed burn.

across all fires. Differences in large dead and down fuel loads (100- and 1000-hour fuels) between treated and untreated stands immediately following wildfire were also negligible. Although not statistically significant, four years following the Oso fire heavy dead and down fuels were greater on untreated stands as charred boles began to rot and fall.

Discussion

Fire Severity and Behavior

The fire behavior triangle states fuel, weather, and topography combine to determine fire behavior. Results indicated fire severity in middle elevation (about 6,400–9,100 ft) southwestern montane coniferous forests was lowered when the fuel leg (surface and aerial fuels) of the fire behavior triangle was reduced by silvicultural activities. In particular, we observed that mechanical treatment followed by prescribed fire (including pile burning) had the greatest influence toward mitigating fire severity. Specifically, as density and basal area decreased and mean tree diameter increased, fire severity decreased. A similar pattern was reported by McHugh and Kolb (2003) in terms of decreased tree mortality (three years following fire) as tree diameters increased from small to intermediate trees. Although a slight increase in tree mortality was reported as intermediate trees increased in diameter to large trees, it was concluded that interactions between crown and bole char damage largely influenced tree mortality (McHugh and Kolb 2003). Our analysis did not indicate mean height to live crown as the most important factor in predicting crown damage. Arguably, this is to be expected as mean height to live crown is not equivalent to canopy base height (Scott and Reinhardt 2001), a variable often cited as a key predictor in crownfire models (Van Wagner 1977; Scott 2003).

Canopy bulk density is known to be a limiting factor affecting crownfire initiation and propagation (Van Wagner 1977; Rothermel 1991). An upper threshold in CBD (> 0.047 kg/m^3, as calculated using FFE-FVS) was observed on mechanically treated stands that included broadcast fire or pile burning (slope was 0–10 %). Two lop and scatter stands had CBDs below 0.047 kg/m^3, and although they did not exhibit crownfire or torching, crowns were completely scorched. A third lop and scatter stand with a CBD calculated at 0.084 kg/m^3 experienced torching. One untreated stand had a calculated CBD of 0.052 kg/m^3. This particular stand experienced a combination of crown scorch, torching, and in some cases crowning. The remaining untreated stands had CBDs ≥ 0.075 kg/m^3 and all experienced near 100% crowning. The idea of empirically derived

USDA For. Serv. Res. Pap. RMRS-RP-55. 2006

11

CBD thresholds limiting or changing crownfire behavior is not new (Agee 1996). Following a 1994 wildfire in the Wenatchee National Forest, Washington, CBDs from multiple sites were calculated and related to fire behavior; a CBD threshold of 0.10 kg/m^3 (as calculated following Agee 1996) was reported with crownfire activity likely above the threshold and not below (Agee 1996). Increased empirical data in combination with current theoretical modeling is necessary before specific threshold CBDs can be recommended as targets for use in fuel reduction planning and risk assessment. Further, it is important to remember crownfire potential is not dependent on any one element of the fire behavior triangle, but rather from multiple combinations of fuel, weather, and topography (Scott and Reinhardt 2001).

Silvicultural cutting prescriptions designed to reduce stand susceptibility to crownfire must consider resulting surface fuels following slash treatment, residual tree and stand characteristics, and slope and aspect. Under extreme conditions created by drought, high winds, and suitable topographical conditions, we observed treated forest stands that, although suffering less severe crown and surface damage than adjacent untreated stands, were still subjected to near stand replacement type damage. This was particularly evident on lop and scatter treatments completed 3–4 years before the Rodeo-Chediski fire. However, this illustrates that even under extreme conditions fire severity can be mitigated by surface and aerial fuel reduction. Furthermore, more recent and aggressive silvicultural treatments including prescribed fire may likely have resulted in still less surface and crown damage. Silvicultural treatments can only be expected to change fire behavior within the limits of their prescription (Finney and Cohen 2003). Spatial location and arrangement of fuel reduction treatments in relation to other treatments must also be considered if landscape scale fire hazard reduction is an objective (Finney 2001, 2003).

Ecological Implications

The ecological implications of different fire severities on natural processes are extensive and complex: wildlife behavior (Smith 2000), wildlife habitat (Smith 2000; Brown and Smith 2000), carbon release (Thornley and Cannell 2004), and global warming (Kasischke and others 1995). These are just a few of many complex issues potentially affected by differing fire regimes, frequencies, and intensities. As such, the following discussion seeks to stimulate thoughts about ecosystem responses as well as highlight one basic ecological implication (understory plant cover) above and below which rest many more.

Greater understory cover particularly that of grasses, in combination with less bare soil cover (Oso fire, table 6), suggests a difference in the relative ecological recovery between treated and untreated forest stands up to four years following wildland fire. Further, because silviculturally treated stands experienced less severe fire damage and subsequently less loss of litter and herbaceous loading (table 7), these stands were less susceptible to soil loss and more conducive to residual plant growth and recovery (table 6). This suggested difference in ecological condition may best be illustrated by the continued high percent of bare soil cover in untreated stands up to four years (i.e., Oso fire) following wildland fire (table 6). Extreme fireline intensities and long residual fire times can cause soil damage leading to loss of nutrient stores (Neary and others 1996), potential loss of viable seed (Miller 2000), change in microclimates (Raison 1979), and altered hydrologic soil behavior leading to rapid erosion events (DeBano and others 1996; Ice and others 2004). This type of soil damage was most pronounced in the untreated study sites.

Management Implications

Functioning watersheds in forested landscapes are vital for flood and erosion control and to the sustainability of water supplies essential for stable societal operation. Evidence of impaired watersheds in terms of erosion and sedimentation immediately following extreme wildfire events are obvious, such as those found following the Peñasco fire (Appendix G). Natural resource managers of all perspectives (private, city, state, or federal) with stewardship charges for diverse landscapes and watersheds are increasingly concerned with minimizing the risk of large-scale crownfires in these systems. Whereas in the past multiple resources such as wildlife habitat, wood products, and range condition were managed at the stand level, increasing pressure, particularly at the federal level, is being exerted to manage these ecological functions and renewable resources at the landscape level under the umbrella of sustainable watersheds. Past and present research results suggest mechanical aerial fuel reduction (i.e., reduced canopy bulk density) followed by frequent prescribed fire is well suited as a management tool to restore and sustain entire watersheds and their ecological functions, particularly in pine-grassland forests. Anywhere the fire has to drop to the surface is an area where some trees will survive and some fuel breaks and firefighters will stand a chance. Not to be overlooked, the extra investment (i.e., prescribed fire and pile burning) required to reduce potential slash fuels and years of accumulated dead and down surface fuels is particularly important for maximizing desired watershed functions, and is evident when comparing lop and scatter vs. lop, pile, burn treatments (i.e., Rodeo-Chediski fire) or shelterwood or commercial harvest vs. harvest and burn treatments (i.e., Borrego and Oso fire) in this study (Appendix G). Although specific target prescriptions for density, diameter distribution, and basal area will depend on interactions with other management objectives (for example, stand regeneration strategies), as a general rule one can expect an inverse relationship between the degree of fuel reduction and the likelihood of crownfire initiation and propagation (within the limits of fuel moisture and wind as dictated by weather). However, beyond recognition and agreement of a specific basal area, diameter, or density treatment, a considerable challenge remains in terms of landscape implementation. Recent theoretical research and post fire analysis indicated that random placement of aerial fuel reduction treatments do little on the landscape scale to slow the rate of spread or change the overall behavior of a crownfire (Finney 2001, 2003; Graham 2003). Spatial arrangement of fuel treatments or restoration prescriptions must be scientifically considered.

In addition to reducing the threat of large-acreage crownfires across backcountry watersheds, wildland-urban interface zones and their respective watersheds must be considered as well in fire hazard planning. Wildland-urban interface stakeholders have reason to thoughtfully consider the implications of this study when bearing in mind how to reduce the threat of high-intensity wildland fire within the interface. Foremost within this group includes urban and rural community leaders and planners, land management agency personnel, as well as citizens and homeowners living within wildland-urban interface areas. Within the wildland-urban interface where the priority is elimination of crownfire potential and reduced fire severity, specific prescriptions should consider (1) aggressive reduction in stem density and basal area while allowing for increased mean tree diameters, (2) reduced canopy bulk density and canopy continuity (i.e., via spatial arrangement of trees and their respective crowns), and (3) aggressive reduction of fine surface fuels. Significantly, these treatments also serve numerous other benefits beyond simply reducing stand replacement fire potential.

Because of the integral role of reducing surface fuels in relation to changing fire behavior, managers should be careful not to mislead stakeholders that simply thinning trees without regard to detail will result in reduced fire behavior to a manageable level. For example, as seen in the lop and scatter treatment on the Rodeo-Chediski fire, the simple rearrangement of the fuel loading (i.e., from aerial to surface fuels) technically reduced fire severity and intensity, but ecologically the end result was still complete stand mortality. Within the interface, both aerial and surface fuel conditions must be addressed if the threat of crownfire danger is to be reduced, and fine surface fuels must constantly be maintained at manageable levels, particularly during the high-risk seasons. Depending on site specific circumstances, frequent prescribed fire can often be an effective tool to keep surface fuel loads at a minimum.

Strict adherence to reduced surface fuels within the scope of the wildland-urban interface should not be confused with the goals and objectives of managing watersheds at the landscape scale. For example, following the recommendation by Cohen (2000) for a 131-ft fuel buffer surrounding dwellings as a proactive and effective approach to reducing risk of home loss in the face of an approaching canopy fire, some have naively questioned the need for further forest thinning and management. Arguably, water supplies vital for urban and rural consumption are the most important of many natural resources directly tied to forested watersheds that without proactive rehabilitation management following nearly a century of fuel accumulation are at prime risk for extensive degradation in the event of a large-scale crownfire (Ice and others 2004; Kaufmann and others 1987). Parallel arguments for proactive landscape management in the imminent path of wildfire can be made for habitat diversity (Waltz and others 2003), forage and rangeland condition (Scotter 1980), recreational use, riparian function (Rinne and Neary 1996), loss of carbon sinks (Kasischke and others 1995), wildfire costs (Lynch 2004), and so on. Further, islands of structural survival in the midst of complete landscape consumption following wildfire are a short-term victory few would advertise as a successful means to an end. The long-term setback in terms of lost natural resources outweighs short-term gains in structural protection, particularly when both are attainable via the same ideology, i.e., proactive management.

The objective of fuel reduction in the wildland-urban interface or within a watershed cannot be to "fire proof" the environment, but rather to reduce the likelihood of stand-replacement crownfire, i.e., change fire behavior. In fact, it was attempts at fire proofing Western coniferous forests that largely led to the unsustainable conditions of today's forest. Furthermore, when forest

Table 8. Fire suppression interpretations (Rothermel 1983).

Flame length (ft)	Fireline intensity (btu/ft/s)	Interpretation
<4	<100	Fires can generally be attacked at the head or flanks by persons using hand tools. Hand line should hold the fire.
4–8	100–500	Fires are too intense for direct attack on the head by persons using hand tools. Hand line cannot be relied on to hold fire. Equipment such as dozers, pumpers, and retardant aircraft can be effective.
8–11	500–1,000	Fire may present serious containment problems: torching, crowning, and spotting. Control effort at the head of fire will probably be ineffective.
>11	>1,000	Crowning, spotting, and major fire runs are possible. Control efforts at head of fire are ineffective.

canopies are opened up via mechanical means, fine understory fuels can be expected to increase. The silver lining in increased fine surface fuels is the improved potential and efficiency to use back-burns ahead of a wildland-head fire, not to mention a key ecological role in the symbiotic relationship between fire and pine forests. Backfires burning through fine surface fuels are more effective and efficient in burning out understory fuels as compared to a closed canopy forest with a deep, but compacted, litter understory. Estimates of fireline intensity indicated that hand and dozer lines would have been effective containment techniques in treated stands (table 4, table 8).

The FFE-FVS is another useful tool that may be helpful to land managers and planners in the wildland-urban interface, particularly U.S. Forest Service personnel familiar with its capabilities. FFE-FVS could be used to estimate existing (i.e., pre or post treatment) and future CBDs and thus provide insight on crownfire potential as well as how often aerial fuels will need to be treated to keep CBDs below crownfire hazard thresholds. It is important to emphasize that CBD alone, without explicit knowledge of surface fuels, is unsuitable as an index to crownfire hazard because of the critical role surface fuels play in fire behavior (Van Wagner 1977).

Implications of this study include increased public understanding of the ecological condition of today's southwestern forests and the potential for long-term damage following crownfire, but more importantly the knowledge that proactive management can be successful in reducing crownfire potential and maintaining ecologically sustainability. From the land manager's perspective, published research data can be used to support proactive management in terms of public relations. In addition, results can help managers assess the likelihood of a crownfire event in a specific stand, to understand how wildland fire behaves in treated vs. untreated stands, to understand how treated vs. untreated stands

will respond following fire, and to understand what specific types of silvicultural treatments will best mitigate damage.

References

Agee, J.K. 1996. The influence of forest structure on fire behavior. In: Sherlock, J. chair. Proceedings of the 17th annual forest and vegetation management conference; 1996 January 16–18; Redding, CA: 52–68.

Ahlgren, I.F.; Ahlgren, C.E. 1960. Ecological effects of forest fires. Botanical Review 26:483–533.

Anderson, D.R.; Burnham, K.P.; Thompson, W.L. 2000. Null hypothesis testing: problems, prevalence, and an alternative. Journal of Wildlife Management 64:912–923.

Avery, T.E.; Burkhart, H.E. 1994. Forest measurements. New York: McGraw-Hill. 408 p.

Baker, M.B., Jr.; Ffolliott, P.F.; DeBano, L.F.; Neary, D.G. 2004. Riparian areas of the southwestern United States–hydrology, ecology, and management. Boca Raton, FL: CRC Press. 408 p.

Biswell, H.H. 1959. Man and fire in ponderosa pine in the Sierra Nevada of California. Sierra Club Bulletin 44:44–53.

Biswell, H.H. 1972. Fire ecology in ponderosa pine-grassland. In proceedings of the 12th Annual Tall Timbers Fire Ecology Conference, Lubbock, TX. 12:69–96.

Brown, J.K.; Oberheu, R.D.; Johnston, C.M. 1982. Handbook for inventorying surface fuels and biomass in the interior West. Gen. Tech. Rep. INT-GTR-129. Ogden, UT: U.S. Department of Agriculture, Forest Service, Intermountain Forest and Range Experiment Station. 48 p.

Brown, J.K.; Smith, J.K. editors. 2000. Wildland fire in ecosystems: effects of fire on flora. Gen.Tech. Rep. RMRS-GTR-42-Vol. 2. Ogden, UT: U.S. Department of Agriculture, Forest Service, Rocky Mountain Research Station. 257 p.

Campbell, R.E.; Baker, M.B., Jr.; Ffolliott, P.F.; Larson, F.R.; Avery, C.C. 1977. Wildfire effects on a ponderosa pine ecosystem: an Arizona case study. Res. Pap. RM-RP-191. Fort Collins, CO: U.S. Department of Agriculture, Forest Service, Rocky Mountain Forest and Range Experiment Station. 12 p.

Cherry, S. 1998. Statistical tests in publications of The Wildlife Society. Wildlife Society Bulletin 26:947–953.

Cohen, J.D. 2000. Preventing disaster: home ignitability in the wildland-urban interface. Journal of Forestry 98(3):15–21.

Cooper, C.F. 1960. Changes in vegetation, structure, and growth of southwestern pine forest since white settlement. Ecological Monographs 30:129–164.

Cooper, C.F. 1961. Patterns in ponderosa pine forests. Ecology 42:493–499.

Covington, W.W.; Moore, M.M. 1994. Southwestern ponderosa forest structure: changes since Euro American settlement. Journal of Forestry 92:39–47.

Cumming, J.A. 1964. Effectiveness of prescribed burning in reducing wildfire damage during periods of abnormally high fire danger. Journal of Forestry 62:535–537.

Davis, L.S.; Cooper, R.W. 1963. How prescribed burning affects wildfire occurrence. Journal of Forestry 61:915–917.

Daniel, C.; Wood, F.S. 1980. Fitting equations to data. 2nd edition. New York: John Wiley & Sons. 458 p.

DeBano, L.F.; Ffolliott, P.F.; Baker, M.B., Jr. 1996. Fire severity effects on water resources. In: Ffolliott, P.F.; DeBano, L.F.; Baker, M.B., Jr.; Gottfried, G.J.; Solis-Garza, G.; Edminster, C.B.; Neary, D.G.; Allen, L.S.; Hamre, R.H. technical coordinators. Effects of fire on Madrean Province ecosystems: a symposium proceedings; 1996 March 11–15; Tucson, AZ. Gen. Tech. Rep. RM-GTR-289. Fort Collins, CO: U.S. Department of Agriculture, Forest Service, Rocky Mountain Forest and Range Experiment Station: 77–84.

Dieterich, J.M. 1980. Chimney Spring forest fire history. Res. Pap. RM-220. Fort Collins, CO: U.S. Department of Agriculture, Forest Service, Rocky Mountain Forest and Range Experiment Station. 8 p.

Fernandes, P.M.; Botelho, H.S. 2003. A review of prescribed burning effectiveness in fire hazard reduction. International Journal of Wildland Fire 12:117–128.

Finney, M.A. 2001. Design of regular landscape fuel treatment patterns for modifying fire growth and behavior. Forest Science 47:219–228.

Finney, M.A. 2003. Calculating fire spread rates across random landscapes. International Journal of Wildland Fire 12:167–174.

Finney, M.A.; Cohen, J.D. 2003. Expectation and evaluation of fuel management objectives. In: Omi, P.N.; Joyce, L.A. technical editors. Fire, fuel treatments, and ecological restoration: conference proceedings; 2002 April 16–18; Fort Collins, CO. Proc. RMRS-P-29. Fort Collins, CO: U.S. Department of Agriculture, Forest Service, Rocky Mountain Research Station: 353–366.

Fulé, P.Z.; McHugh, C.W.; Heinlein, T.A.; Covington, W.W. 2001. Potential fire behavior is reduced following forest restoration treatments. In: Vance, R.K.; Edminster, C.B.; Covington, W.W.; Blake, J.A. compilers. Ponderosa pine ecosystems restoration and conservation: steps toward stewardship; 2000 April 25–27; Flagstaff, AZ. Proc. RMRS-P-22. Ogden, UT: U.S. Department of Agriculture, Forest Service, Rocky Mountain Research Station: 28–35.

Graham, R.T.; Harvey, A.E.; Jain, T.B.; Tonn, J.R. 1999. The effects of thinning and similar stand treatments on fire behavior in Western Forests. Gen. Tech. Rep. PNW-GTR-463. Portland, OR: U.S. Department of Agriculture, Forest Service, Pacific Northwest Research Station. 27 p.

Graham, R.T. technical editor. 2003. Hayman fire case study: summary. Gen. Tech. Rep. RMRS-GTR-115. Ogden, UT: U.S. Department of Agriculture, Forest Service, Rocky Mountain Research Station. 32 p.

Graham, R.T.; McCaffery, S.; Jain, T.B. technical editors. 2004. Science basis for changing forest structure to modify wildfire behavior and severity. Gen. Tech. Rep. RMRS-GTR-120. Fort Collins, CO: U.S. Department of Agriculture, Forest Service, Rocky Mountain Research Station. 43 p.

Gray, K.L.; Reinhardt, E.D. 2003. Analysis of algorithms for predicting canopy fuel; 2003 November 16–20; Orlando, FL. 2nd International Wildland Fire Ecology and Management Congress. American Meteorological Society.

Habeck, J.R. 1990. Old-growth ponderosa pine-western larch forest in western Montana: ecology and management. The Northwest Environmental Journal 6:271–292.

Ice, G.G.; Neary, D.G.; Adams, P.W. 2004. Effects of wildfire on soils and watershed processes. Journal of Forestry 102(6): 16–20.

Incident Response Pocket Guide. 2004. A publication of the National Wildfire Coordinating Group. Available: http://www.nwcg.gov/ [May 2005].

Johnson, D.H. 1999. The insignificance of statistical significance testing. Journal of Wildlife Management 63:763–772.

Lynch, D.L. 2004. What do forest fires really cost? Journal of Forestry 102(6):42–49.

Kasischke, E.S.; Christensen, N.L., Jr.; Stocks, B.J. 1995. Fire, global warming, and the carbon balance of boreal forests. Ecological Applications 5:437–451.

Kaufmann, M.R.; Troendle, C.A.; Ryan, M.G.; Mowrer, H.T. 1987. Trees – the link between silviculture and hydrology. Gen. Tech. Rep. RM-GTR-149. Fort Collins, CO: U.S. Department of Agriculture, Forest Service, Rocky Mountain Forest and Range Experiment Station: 54–60.

Mallows, C.L. 1964. Some comments on C_p. Technometrics 15:661–675.

McHugh, C.W.; Kolb, T.E. 2003. Ponderosa pine mortality following fire in northern Arizona. International Journal of Wildland Fire 12:7–22.

Miller, M. 2000. Fire autecology. In: Brown, J.K.; Smith, J.K. editors. 2000. Wildland fire in ecosystems: effects of fire on flora. Gen. Tech. Rep. RMRS-GTR-42-Vol. 2. Ogden, UT: U.S. Department of Agriculture, Forest Service, Rocky Mountain Research Station: 9–34.

Moir, W.H.; Geils, B.; Benoit, M.A.; Scurlock, D. 1997. Ecology of southwestern ponderosa pine forests. In: Block, W.M.; Finch, D.M. technical editors. Songbird ecology in southwestern ponderosa pine forests: a literature review. Gen. Tech. Rep. RM-GTR-292. Fort Collins, CO: U.S. Department of Agriculture, Forest Service, Rocky Mountain Forest and Range Experiment Station: 3–27.

Moore, E.B.; Smith, G.E.; Little, S. 1955. Wildfire damage reduced on prescribed-burned areas in New Jersey. Journal of Forestry 53:339–341.

Mueller-Dombois, D.; Ellenberg, H. 1974. Aims and methods of vegetation ecology. New York: John Wiley and Sons. 547 p.

Neary, D.G.; Overby, S.A.; Gottfried, G.J.; Perry, H.M. 1996. Nutrients in fire-dominated ecosystems. In: Ffolliott, P.F.; DeBano, L.F.; Baker, M.B., Jr.; Gottfried, G.J.; Solis-Garza, G.; Edminster, C.B.; Neary, D.G.; Allen, L.S.; Hamre, R.H. technical coordinators. Effects of fire on Madrean Province ecosystems: symposium proceedings; 1996 March 11–15; Tucson, AZ. Gen. Tech. Rep. RM-GTR-289. Fort Collins, CO. U.S. Department of Agriculture, Forest Service, Rocky Mountain Forest and Range Experiment Station: 107–117.

Omi, P.N.; Kalabokidis, K.D. 1991. Fire damage on extensively versus intensively managed forest stands within the North Fork fire, 1988. Northwest Science 65:149–157.

Omi, P.N.; Martinson, E. 2002. Effect of fuels treatment on wildfire severity. Final report submitted to the Joint Fire Science Program Governing Board.

Pollet, J.; Omi, P.N. 2002. Effect of thinning and prescribed burning on crownfire severity in ponderosa pine forests. International Journal of Wildland Fire 11:1–10.

Pyne, S.J. 1982. Fire in America: a cultural history of wildland and rural fire. New Jersey: Princeton University Press. 654 p.

Pyne, S.J. 1996. Nouvelle Southwest. In: Covington, W.W.; Wagner, P.K. technical coordinators. Conference on adaptive ecosystem restoration and management: restoration of Cordilleran conifer landscapes of North America; 1996 June 6–8; Flagstaff, AZ. Gen. Tech. Rep. RM-GTR-278. Fort Collins, CO: U.S. Department of Agriculture, Forest Service, Rocky Mountain Forest and Range Experiment Station: 10–16.

Pyne, S.J.; Andrews, P.L.; Laven, R.D. 1996. Introduction to wildland fire. New York: John Wiley and Sons. 769 p.

Raison, R.J. 1979. Modification of the soil environment by vegetation fires, with particular reference to nitrogen transformations: a review. Plant and Soil 51:73–108.

Reinhardt, E.D.; Crookston, N.L. 2003. The fire and fuels extension to the forest vegetation simulator. Gen. Tech. Rep. RMRS-GTR-116. Ogden, UT: U.S. Department of Agriculture, Forest Service, Rocky Mountain Research Station. 209 p.

Rinne, J.N.; Neary, D.G. 1996. Fire effects on aquatic habitats and biota in Madrean-type ecosystems: Southwestern United States. In: Ffolliott, P.F.; DeBano, L.F.; Baker, M.B., Jr.; Gottfried, G.J.; Solis-Garza, G.; Edminster, C.B.; Neary, D.G.; Allen, L.S.; Hamre, R.H. technical coordinators. Effects of fire on Madrean Province ecosystems: a symposium proceedings; 1996 March 11–15; Tucson, AZ. Gen. Tech. Rep. RM-GTR-289. Fort Collins, CO. U.S. Department of Agriculture, Forest Service, Rocky Mountain Forest and Range Experiment Station: 135–145.

Ryan, K.C.; Noste, N.V. 1985. Evaluating prescribed fires. In: Lotan, J.E.; Kilgore, B.M.; Fischer, W.C.; Mutch, R.W. technical coordinators. Proceedings: symposium and workshop on wilderness fire; 1983 November 15–18; Missoula, MT. Gen. Tech. Rep. INT-182. Ogden, UT: U.S. Department of Agriculture, Forest Service, Intermountain Forest and Range Experiment Station: 230–238.

Rothermel, R.C. 1983. How to predict the spread and intensity of forest and range fires. Gen. Tech. Rep. INT-143. Ogden, UT: U.S. Department of Agriculture, Forest Service, Intermountain Forest and Range Experiment Station. 161 p.

Rothermel, R.C. 1991. Predicting behavior and size of crown fires in the Northern Rocky Mountains. Res. Pap. INT-RP-438. Ogden, UT: U.S. Department of Agriculture, Forest Service, Intermountain Forest and Range Experiment Station. 46 p.

Sackett, S.; Haase, S.; Harrington, M.G. 1993. Restoration of southwestern ponderosa pine ecosystems with fire. In: Covington, W.W.; DeBano, L.F. technical coordinators. Sustainable ecological systems: implementing an ecological approach to land management. Gen. Tech. Rep. RM-247. Fort Collins, CO: U.S. Department of Agriculture Forest Service, Rocky Mountain Forest and Range Experiment Station: 115–121.

Sando, R.W.; Wick, C.H. 1972. A method of evaluating crown fuels in forest stands. Res. Pap. NC-84. Saint Paul, MN: U.S. Department of Agriculture, Forest Service, North Central Forest and Range Experiment Station. 10 p.

SAS Institute. 1985. SAS user's guide: statistics. 5th edition. North Carolina: SAS Institute. 956 p.

Schubert, G.H. 1974. Silviculture of southwestern ponderosa pine: the status of our knowledge. Res. Pap. RM-RP-123. Fort Collins, CO: U.S. Department of Agriculture, Forest Service, Rocky Mountain Forest and Range Experiment Station. 71 p.

Scott, J.H. 1998. Fuel reduction in residential and scenic forests: a comparison of three treatments in a western Montana ponderosa pine stand. Res. Pap. RMRS-RP-5. Fort Collins, CO: U.S. Department of Agriculture, Forest Service, Rocky Mountain Research Station. 19 p.

Scott, J.H. 2003. Canopy fuel treatment standards for the wildland-urban interface. In: Omi, P.N.; Joyce, L.A. technical editors. Fire, fuel treatments, and ecological restoration: conference proceedings; 2002 April 16–18; Fort Collins, CO. Proc. RMRS-P-29. Fort Collins, CO: U.S. Department of Agriculture, Forest Service, Rocky Mountain Research Station: 29–37.

Scott, J.H.; Reinhardt, E.D. 2001. Assessing crownfire potential by linking models of surface and crownfire behavior. Res. Pap. RMRS-RP-29. Fort Collins, CO: U.S. Department of Agriculture, Forest Service, Rocky Mountain Research Station. 59 p.

Scotter, G.W. 1980. Management of wild ungulate habitat in the Western United States and Canada: a review. Journal of Range Management 33:16–27.

Smith, J.K. editor. 2000. Wildland fire in ecosystems: effects of fire on fauna. Gen. Tech. Rep. RMRS-GTR-42-Vol. 1. Ogden, UT: U.S. Department of Agriculture, Forest Service, Rocky Mountain Research Station. 83 p.

Thornley, J.M.; Cannell, M.R. 2004. Long-term effects of fire frequency on carbon storage and productivity of boreal forests: a modeling study. Tree Physiology 24:765–773.

Van Wagner, R. 1968. Survival of coniferous plantations following fires in Los Angeles County. Journal of Forestry 66:622–625.

Van Wagner, C.E. 1973. Height of crown scorch in forest fires. Canadian Journal of Forest Research 3:373–378.

Van Wagner, C.E. 1977. Conditions for the start and spread of crown fire. Canadian Journal of Forestry. 7:23–34.

Wagle, R.F.; Eakle, T.W. 1979. A controlled burn reduces the impact of a subsequent wildfire in a ponderosa pine vegetation type. Forest Science 25:123–129.

Waltz, A.E.M.; Fulé, P.Z.; Covington, W.W.; Moore, M.M. 2003. Diversity in ponderosa pine forest structure following ecological restoration treatments. Forest Science 49:885–900.

Weaver, H. 1943. Fire as an ecological and silvicultural factor in the ponderosa pine region of the Pacific slope. Journal of Forestry 41:7–15.

Weaver, H. 1951. Fire as an ecological factor in the southwestern ponderosa pine forests. Journal of Forestry 49:93–98.

Weaver, H. 1964. Fire and management problems in ponderosa pine. In proceedings of the 3rd Annual Tall Timbers Fire Ecology Conference, Tallahassee, FL. 3:61–79.

Weaver, H. 1967. Fire and its relationship to ponderosa pine. In proceedings of the 7th Annual Tall Timbers Fire Ecology Conference, Tallahassee, FL. 7:127–149.

Woolsey, T.S. 1911. Western yellow pine in Arizona and New Mexico. Bulletin 101. U.S. Department of Agriculture, Forest Service.

Appendix A. Potential study sites.

Listing of all potential study sites (i.e., a silviculturally treated stand subsequently subjected to a wildland fire) visited in the summers of 2002 and 2003 in Arizona and New Mexico (USDA Forest Service Region 3), and reason for exclusion if applicable.

State	National Forest	Fire name and year	Reason for exclusion
Arizona	Apache-Sitgreaves	Rodeo-Chediski 2002	Not applicable
	Coconino	Horseshoe 1996	Salvage cut following fire.
	Coronado	Bullock 2002	Lack of adjacent treated and untreated sites with similar aspect.
	Kaibab	Pumpkin 2000	Lack of adjacent treated and untreated sites with similar slope and aspect.
	Kaibab	Trick 2002	Insufficient acreage in treated and untreated burned area.
	Prescott	Indian 2002	Lack of adjacent treated and untreated sites with similar aspect.
New Mexico	Carson	Valle Grande 1991	Salvage cut
	Cibola	La Jara 1999	Lack of adjacent treated and untreated sites with similar slope and aspect.
	Gila	Middle 2002	Lack of adjacent treated and untreated sites with similar slope and aspect, and insufficient acreage in treated and untreated burned area.
	Lincoln	Kokopelli 2002	Insufficient acreage in treated and untreated burned area.
	Lincoln	Penasco 2002	Not applicable
	Lincoln	Scott Able 2000	Not applicable
	Lincoln	Walker 2003	Lack of adjacent treated and untreated sites with similar slope and aspect, and insufficient acreage in treated and untreated burned area.
	Santa Fe	Borrego 2002	Not applicable
	Santa Fe	Oso 1998	Not applicable
	Socorro BLM	Chance 2000	Lack of adjacent treated and untreated sites with similar slope and aspect.

Appendix B.

Mean and standard error (SE) of forest stand characteristics and measured fire behavior indices important to understanding fire behavior in New Mexico and Arizona National Forests, June–August 2002. Mode value is reported for surface and crown damage. (Non-replicated stand data)

	Fire and treatment[a]											
	Peñasco (Coleman One)				Peñasco (Coleman Two)				Scott Able			
	Commercial thin		UT		Commercial thin		UT		Shelterwood		UT	
Variable	$\bar{x}$	SE	$\bar{x}$	SE	$\bar{x}$	SE	$\bar{x}$	SE	$\bar{x}$	SE	$\bar{x}$	SE
Estimated pre-fire condition												
Basal area (ft²/ac)	60	23	128	15	13	3	127	23	30	13	134	14
Diameter at breast height (in)	13	1	13	1	20	1	16	1	16	3	18	1
Density (stems/ac)	109	67	253	68	6	1	182	46	16	4	148	29
Height to live crown (ft)	14	5	38	1	42	6	47	3	47	7	25	2
Canopy bulk density (kg/m³)	0.072	0.04	0.259	0.08	0.006	0.01	0.090	0.02	0.018	0.01	0.196	0.06
Fire severity												
Surface damage (0–3)	2		3		1		3		1		2	
Crown damage (0–4)	3		4		2		4		1		4	
Fire behavior												
Height bole char (ft)	25	9	63	3	21	2	69	5	8	2	56	3
Fireline intensity (btu/ft/s)[b]	522	58	602+	34	378	194	650+	28	118	31	658+	36

[a] UT = untreated.
[b] "+" indicates underestimated fireline intensity.

Appendix C.

Mean and standard error (SE) of understory cover (%) response after wildland fire in New Mexico and Arizona National Forests, June–August 2002. (Non-replicated stand data)

| | Cover type | | | | | | | | | |
| | Grass | | Forb | | Shrub <3.3 ft | | Bare soil | | Litter | |
Treatment	$\bar{x}$	SE	$\bar{x}$	SE	$\bar{x}$	SE	$\bar{x}$	SE	$\bar{x}$	SE
Peñasco Fire 2002: Coleman One										
Commercial thin	<1	0.1	0	0.0	<1	<0.1	82	2.5	19.2	2.1
Untreated	0	0.0	0	0.0	0	0.0	91	1.1	3.1	0.3
Peñasco Fire 2002: Coleman Two										
Commercial thin	2	0.7	1	0.2	0	0.0	66	4.8	26.5	4.6
Untreated	<1	0.1	0	0.0	0	0.0	78	8.2	19.7	8.8
Scott Able Fire 2000										
Shelterwood	29	2.3	5	1.1	4	1.8	42	2.3	15.0	2.6
Untreated	<1	0.3	3	0.9	<1	0.2	70	3.1	13.8	2.3

USDA For. Serv. Res. Pap. RMRS-RP-55. 2006

19

Appendix D.

Mean and standard error (SE) of fuel loading and depth in treated and untreated forest stands following wildland fire in New Mexico and Arizona National Forests June–August 2002. (Non-replicated stand data)

	Fire and treatment[a]											
	Peñasco (Coleman One)[b]				Peñasco (Coleman Two)[b]				Scott Able			
	Commercial		UT		Commercial		UT		Shelterwood		UT	
Variable	x̄	SE	x̄	SE	x̄	SE	x̄	SE	x̄	SE	x̄	SE
Herb loading (lbs/ac)	<1	<1	0	0	23	11	0	0	183	32	29	10
Litter loading (lbs/ac)	840	198	74	39	1,052	238	450	187	832	272	679	156
1-hr fuel loading (tons/ac)	NA		NA		<0.1	<0.1	0.0	0.0	0.1	<0.1	0.1	<0.1
10-hr fuel loading (tons/ac)	NA		NA		0.4	<0.1	0.1	0.1	0.6	0.1	0.4	0.1
100-hr fuel loading (tons/ac)	NA		NA		0.3	0.3	0.3	0.2	1.9	0.5	0.4	0.2
1000-hr fuel loading (tons/ac)	NA		NA		0.4	0.2	2.2	1.0	12.1	4.1	7.9	4.5
Litter depth (in)	0.1	<0.1	<0.1	0.1	0.2	<0.1	0.1	<0.1	0.3	0.1	0.1	<0.1
Duff depth (in)	0.0	0.0	0.0	0.0	<0.1	<0.1	0.0	0.0	0.2	0.1	0.1	<0.1

[a] UT = untreated
[b] NA = Not available

Appendix E.

Mean surface (modified after Ryan and Noste 1985) and crown damage (Omi and Kalabokidis 1991) severity index for treated and untreated stands (standard error bars included). Data summarized by fire for New Mexico study sites, June–August 2002. (Non-replicated stand data)

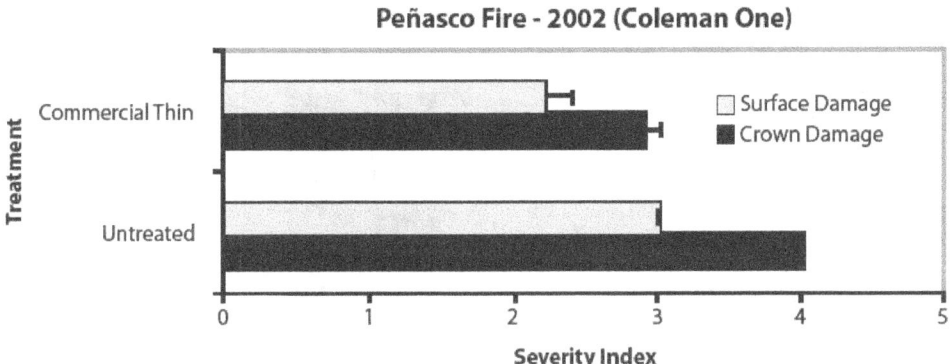

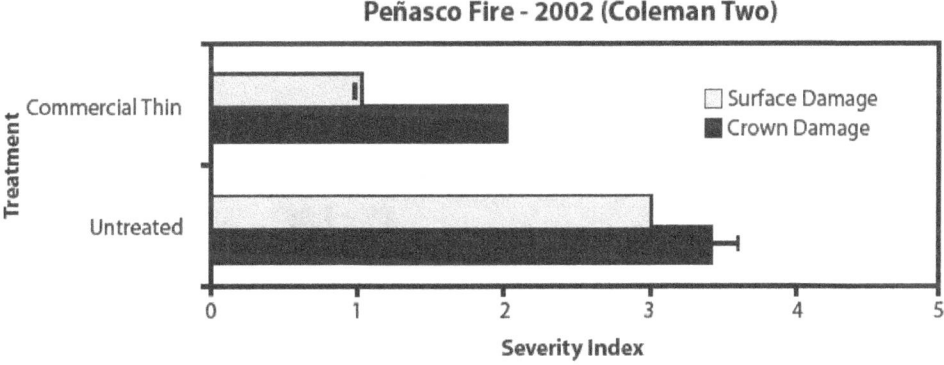

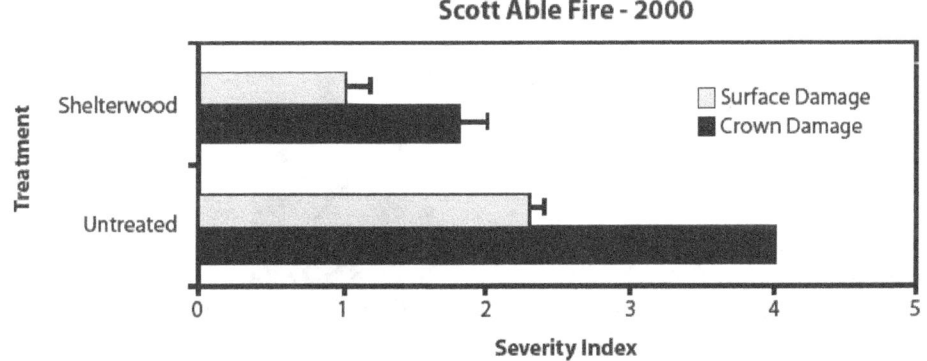

Appendix F.

Percent (%) of treated and untreated tree canopies scorched (i.e., needles remaining) and consumed (i.e., no needles remaining) by wildland fire (standard error bars included). Data summarized by fire for New Mexico study sites, June–August 2002. (Non-replicated stand data)

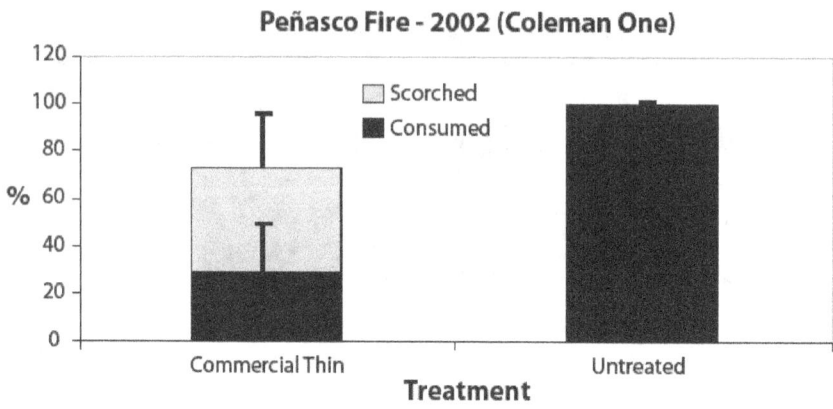

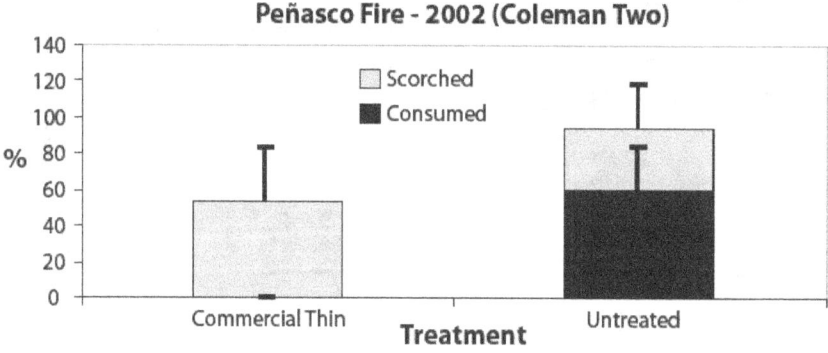

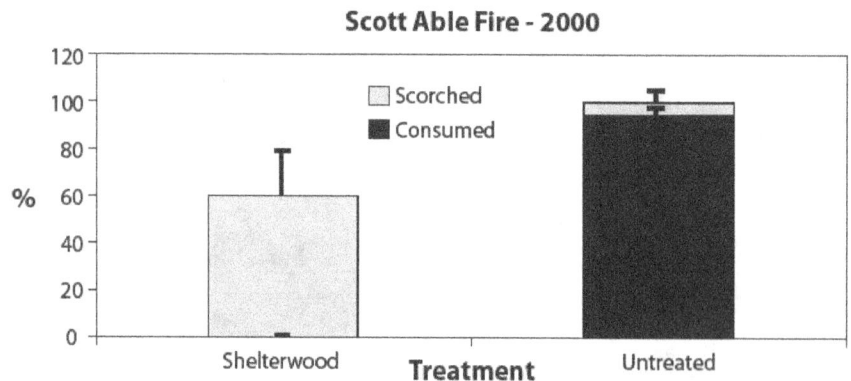

22

USDA For. Serv. Res. Pap. RMRS-RP-55. 2006

Appendix G.

Rodeo-Chediski Fire 2002, Apache-Sitgreaves National Forest, Bagnal study site. Pictures taken two weeks after fire, spring 2002. Canopy bulk density (CBD) calculated using FFE-FVS.

Lop, pile, burn.
Stand CBD: 0.034 kg/m^3

Lop and scatter.
Stand CBD: 0.035 kg/m^3

Untreated.
Stand CBD: 0.111 kg/m^3

USDA For. Serv. Res. Pap. RMRS-RP-55. 2006

23

Appendix G *continued.*

Borrego Fire 2002, Santa Fe National Forest. Pictures taken one year after fire, summer 2003. Canopy bulk density (CBD) calculated using FFE-FVS.

Commercial harvest with prescribed burn.
Medio study site.
Stand CBD: 0.018 kg/m³

Untreated.
Medio study site.
Stand CBD: 0.052 kg/m³

Commercial harvest with prescribed burn.
Ponderosa Park study site.
Stand CBD: 0.021 kg/m³

Untreated.
Ponderosa Park study site.
Stand CBD: 0.118 kg/m³

Appendix G *continued.*

Oso Fire 1998, Santa Fe National Forest. Pictures taken four years after fire, summer 2002. Canopy bulk density (CBD) calculated using FFE-FVS.

Commercial harvest with prescribed burn.
Terrero study site.
Stand CBD: 0.037 kg/m

Untreated.
Terrero study site.
Stand CBD: 0.129 kg/m^3

Commercial harvest with prescribed burn.
Ojito study site.
Stand CBD: 0.016 kg/m^3

Untreated.
Ojito study site.
Stand CBD: 0.109 kg/m^3

USDA For. Serv. Res. Pap. RMRS-RP-55. 2006

25

Appendix G *continued.*

Peñasco Fire 2002, Lincoln National Forest. Pictures taken two months after fire, spring 2002. Canopy bulk density (CBD) calculated using FFE-FVS.

Commercial thin (picture taken after salvage cut).
Coleman One study site.
Stand CBD: 0.110 kg/m^3

Untreated.
Coleman One study site.
Stand CBD: 0.099 kg/m^3

Commercial thin.
Coleman Two study site.
Stand CBD: 0.003 kg/m^3
(Photo perspective: 180 degrees from adjacent photo)

Untreated.
Coleman Two study site.
Stand CBD: 0.070 kg/m^3

Appendix G *continued.*

Scott Able Fire 2000, Lincoln National Forest, Wayland study site. Pictures taken two years after fire, spring 2002. Canopy bulk density (CBD) calculated using FFE-FVS.

Shelterwood.
Stand CBD: 0.056 kg/m^3
Note difference in surface cover between two photos.

Untreated.
Stand CBD: 0.130 kg/m^3

USDA For. Serv. Res. Pap. RMRS-RP-55. 2006

27

Appendix G *continued.*

Peñasco Fire 2002, Lincoln National Forest. Pictures taken after first thundershower following fire, spring 2002.

Upper retention dam after first thundershower following fire (notice spillway overflow).

Lower retention dam after first thundershower following fire (no spillway overflow).

Trash rack and silt dam before (above) and after (right) first thundershower following fire.

USDA For. Serv. Res. Pap. RMRS-RP-55. 2006